The GIFT of EUCHARIST

AUTHORS

Rev. Richard N. Fragomeni

Jean Marie Hiesberger

The Ad Hoc Committee to Oversee the Use of the Catechism, National Conference of Catholic Bishops, has found this catechetical text to be in conformity with the Catechism of the Catholic Church.

RCL Benziger

Allen, Texas

Nihil Obstat
Kathleen Flanagan, S.C. Ph.D

Imprimatur
† Most Reverend Frank J. Rodimer
Bishop of Paterson

December 16, 1998

The *nihil obstat* and *imprimatur* are official declaration that a book or pamphlet is free of doctrinal and moral error. No implication is contained therein that those who have granted the *nihil obstat* and *imprimatur* agree with the contents, opinions, or statements expressed.

Send all inquiries to:
RCL Benziger
206 East Bethany Drive
Allen, Texas 75002-3804

Toll Free   877-275-4725
Fax   800-688-8356

Visit us at www.RCLBenziger.com

Printed in the United States of America

S6702   ISBN 978-0-7829-1292-0

19 20 21 22 23 • 13 12 11 10 09

Acknowledgments

Contributing Writer: Anne E. Neuberger

Theological Reviewer: Nathan Mitchell

All adaptations of Scripture are based on the *New American Bible* with Revised New Testament and Psalms. Copyright © 1991, 1986, 1970. Confraternity of Christian Doctrine, Inc. Washington, D.C. All rights reserved. No part of the *New American Bible* may be reprinted without permission in writing from the copyright holder.

Excepts from the English translation of *The Roman Missal* © 1973, International Committee on English in the Liturgy, Inc (ICEL)

Art Credits

Cover art: Nancy Tobin

Scripture art: Margaret Sanfilippo

All other art: 1: Jean and Mou-Sien Tseng. 2–3: Anni Matsick. 8: Bob Berry. 11–13: Jean and Mou-Sien Tseng. 18: Terry Taylor. 19: Bernard Adnet. 21: Jean and Mou-Sien Tseng. 28: Mike Radencich. 28–29, 31: Jean and Mou-Sien Tseng. 33: Sally Springer. 41: Jean and Mou-Sien Tseng. 42–43: t. Roger Roth. 43: l. Anni Matsick. 48–49: Anni Matsick. 51: Jean and Mou-Sien Tseng. 58: Jean and Mou-Sien Tseng. 59: Bob Berry. 61–63: Jean and Mou-Sien Tseng. 68: Anni Matsick. 71: Jean and Mou-Sien Tseng. 78–79: Jean and Mou-Sien Tseng. 84: Anni Matsick. Logos/borders: Nancy Tobin.

Photo Credits

1: tl Lee F. Snyder/Photo Researchers, Inc.; bl © John Eastcott/Yva Momatuik/Woodfin Camp & Associates; tr Peter Correz/Tony Stone Images. 2: Esbin-Anderson/The Image Works. 6: tl A.K.G. Berlin/Superstock. 9: t. John Eastcott/Yva Momatiuk/Photo Researchers, Inc.; b Gale Zucker/Stock Boston. 11: r Bob Daemmrich/Stock Boston; l. Paul Barton/The Stock Market. 16, 27: Fr. Gene Plaisted/The Crosiers. 17: Myrleen Ferguson/PhotoEdit. 21: tr Bob Daemmrich/Stock Boston; l Ed Bock/The Stock Market. 22: Jose Luis Banus/FPG International. 26: Jim Whitmer Photography. 27: Michael Newman/PhotoEdit. 36: Michael Newman/PhotoEdit. 37: Fr. Gene Plaisted/The Crosiers. 38: Jim Whitmer Photography. 39: l Myrleen Ferguson/PhotoEdit; m Fr. Gene Plaisted/The Crosiers. 40: Myrleen Ferguson/PhotoEdit. 42: t Tony Freeman/PhotoEdit. 46: J. Gerard Smith/PhotoEdit. 47: l Cleo Freelance Photography; r Tony Freeman/PhotoEdit. 51: t. Jonathan Blair/© National Geographic Society; bl Stephen McBrady/PhotoEdit; br Bruce Dale/© National Geographic Society. 52: David Young-Wolff/PhotoEdit. 56: Fr. Gene Plaisted/The Crosiers. 57: l Fr. Gene Plaisted/The Crosiers; r JimWhitmer Photography. 62: l. Lawrence Migdale/Stock Boston; r. Tony Freeman/PhotoEdit. 63: l Sandy King/The Image Bank; r Myrleen Ferguson/PhotoEdit. 67: l Michael Newman/PhotoEdit; r Jose Carillo/PhotoEdit. 72, 73: Elliot Smith for Silver Burdett Ginn. 80: tl, br Fr. Gene Plaisted/The Crosiers; tr Myrleen Ferguson/PhotoEdit. 85: Richard Hutchings for SBG. 90: J. Gerard Smith for SBG.

Contents

As I prepare to celebrate the sacrament of Eucharist, I will let the Holy Spirit open my heart to all of God's wonderful gifts, especially the gift of his Son, Jesus Christ. I will learn how to give God thanks and praise with my parish community and the rest of the Church.

_____

Child

∽∽◇∽∽

I, too, will let the Holy Spirit open my heart to all of God's wonderful gifts, especially the gift of his Son, Jesus Christ. I will support this child through my prayers and my presence as, together with our parish community, we celebrate the abundant life that the Lord gives us.

_____

Family Member

Let's Give Thanks and Praise

The sacrament of the Eucharist is a wonderful gift from Jesus Christ, our risen Lord. This gift of Eucharist is so amazing that we are driven to give thanks from the depths of our souls. We're all familiar with the power of gratitude in our daily lives. With your child, recall experiences of thankfulness by writing or drawing about something that makes you feel thankful.

Let's Give Thanks and Praise

Do you like getting gifts? Most people do. Some people feel special when they receive a gift. Others feel happy.

When you receive a gift, how do you feel?

What is the best gift you ever received? Write a story about it. If you want, choose words from the list to complete your story.

delighted	treasure	excited	keep
beautiful	amazed	colorful	tiny
remember	precious	large	love
surprised	pleased	care for	

Once I was given a gift, my favorite gift.

It was _____,

and it was _____.

I was _____!

_____ gave

me this wonderful gift. I will always

_____ it.

The Birth of Jesus

The sheep dozed and the shepherds watched in the cold night. Then, a bright light shone all around them, and a magnificent, smiling angel appeared.

The shepherds cried out in fear, but the angel said, "Do not be afraid. I bring you great joy for the whole world! Today a savior, Christ the Lord, has been born. God's son has been given to you. Rejoice!"

The whole sky filled with angels, surrounding the shepherds with their happiness. The angels sang joyfully, "Glory to God!"

The shepherds hurried to see Baby Jesus. Then they told everyone about the angels and about Jesus, a gift from God to us.

All the way back to their sheep, the shepherds laughed and shouted their praises to God, for they were filled with joy.

Based on Luke 2:8–20

5

Jesus, God's Greatest Gift

Christ and the Children Nolde, Emil. 1867-1956. German. Museum of Modern Art, New York City.

God, our loving Father, gives us many wonderful gifts: the sun, the moon, plants, animals, and one another. But God's greatest gift is Jesus, his only Son. Jesus is both God and man. He became like us to save us from our sins and teach us how to give thanks and praise to his Father.

Jesus healed people who were ill and cared about people who were poor. He forgave those who did wrong and hurt others.

Jesus loved everyone and asked them to be kind and forgive one another. Jesus lived for us, he died for us, and he rose again to life for us.

Jesus is still with us. He still shows us the love that God pours out for us. Jesus brings us closer to God, who made us to know him, love him, and praise him. We are thankful to God for Jesus, his Son.

Draw something here that you know about Jesus.

Jesus forgave our sins.
Jesus care and love for us.
Jesus heal people.
Jesus was kind to people
Jesus teach us, how to
Thank and praise.

7

Gifts for Us

God gives us so much that we feel blessed. We feel joyful and loved. We want to thank and praise God every day.

Sometimes, Jesus went to a quiet place to praise and thank his Father. You can do this, too. Close your eyes. Go to a quiet, holy place inside of you. Feel the warm or cool air you breathe. Wait for a feeling of quiet happiness or calmness within you. Even without seeing God, you can feel him with you always.

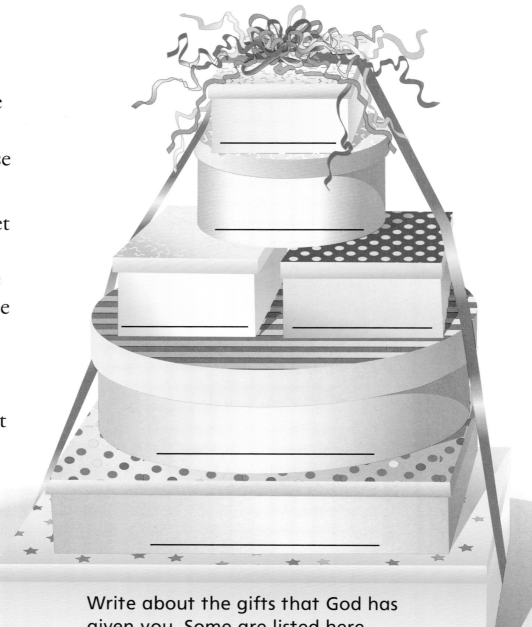

Write about the gifts that God has given you. Some are listed here.

life   world   Jesus   food   people

8

A Thank-you Prayer

God, our loving Father,

thank you for _____,

and _____,

and _____.

You show your love to us every day.

Thank you, God!

Amen.

Family Time

Pray the prayer on this page with your child every night.

We Believe

- ☐ God made us to know him, love him, and praise him.
- ☐ God loves us so much that he gives us many gifts.
- ☐ God gives us his greatest gift, Jesus.
- ☐ We can thank and praise God every day.

We Remember and Celebrate

Leader: **For brother sun, who brings us light.**
Bring your arms together over your head for the sun.

All: **Be praised, my Lord!**

Leader: **For sister moon and the stars who bring us night.**
Make a sweeping motion for the night sky.

All: **Be praised, my Lord!**

Leader: **For sister water, who cools our thirst.**
Make a pouring motion.

All: **Be praised, my Lord!**

Leader: **For mother earth, who feeds and shelters us.**
Pat the floor, then stand up and open your arms.

All: **Be praised, my Lord!**

Based on the Canticle of the Sun

Let's Celebrate

Every day has its holy moments, snippets of time when we stand in wonder at God's love in our lives. But to appreciate such moments, we have to notice them first. Sometimes they slip by too quickly. Talk with your child about such times. What does he or she notice about those instances when God seems near?

In the space, trace the outline of your child's hand. Then on and around the hand, write or draw about moments when family members can be aware of God touching their lives.

Let's Celebrate

"I will add the flour, Joel," Cora said. "This will be one super, terrific, amazing cake!"

Joel smiled. Cora was a neighbor, yet like family. She always said "super, terrific, amazing" about everything: cakes, sunsets, songs, and even Joel himself.

"Now the eggs!" she declared.

Dad went to the airport to pick up Grandma. Mom ironed a dress for Joel's sister. Joel's cousin stirred a pot of soup. Karen put flowers in a vase.

"This will be one super, terrific, amazing cake," Cora said again. "And we will feast and sing!"

What do you think Joel and his family are celebrating? _____

_____

_____

What special times do you enjoy celebrating?

_____

_____

_____

More Than Enough

"**W**here can we buy bread for these people?"

Jesus spoke to Philip as they looked out at the huge crowd of people. The people had come to be with Jesus. There were thousands!

"Two hundred days of wages would not buy enough food!" Philip answered.

"A boy has five loaves of bread and two fish," Andrew said. "But that is nothing in this crowd."

"Have the people sit on the ground," Jesus told them.

Jesus took the bread and the fish. Looking up to heaven, he blessed and broke them. He gave them to the disciples for the people.

All the women, children, and men ate. When they were finished and no one was hungry, there were still twelve baskets of food left!

Based on John 6:1–14

15

The Goodness of God

Jesus calls the community of his followers to give thanks to his Father. We became Jesus' followers at Baptism. We especially remember we are God's people when we give thanks at the Eucharist.

The Eucharist is one of the sacraments of initiation. A sacrament is a most special celebration. It is an action of Christ who comes to us in the Church through the power of the Holy Spirit.

The word <u>Eucharist</u> means "giving thanks." We also call our celebration the Mass.

Baptism and Confirmation are sacraments of initiation, too. In Baptism we are welcomed into the family of Jesus' followers, the Church.

In Confirmation the Holy Spirit helps us to follow Jesus even more closely. In the celebration of Eucharist we thank God for the gift of Jesus.

So we go to church to marvel at the blessings God gives to us. Before we receive the gift of Jesus for the first time, we receive forgiveness in the sacrament of Reconciliation.

An Invitation for You

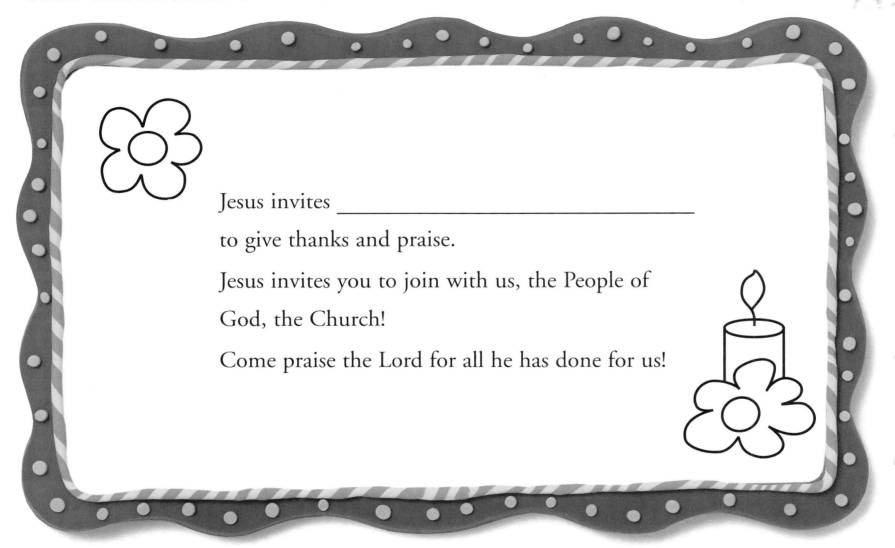

Jesus invites _____

to give thanks and praise.

Jesus invites you to join with us, the People of God, the Church!

Come praise the Lord for all he has done for us!

Create an invitation to Mass. Decorate it, making it colorful and joyous. Make it special, for it is your very own invitation to take part in the celebration of the Eucharist often!

In the spaces, write words you know that tell about the celebration of the Eucharist.

Celebration of the Eucharist

We Believe

☐ We are the People of God, the Church.

☐ We gather together to thank and praise God in the celebration of the Eucharist, also called the Mass.

☐ The word <u>Eucharist</u> means "giving thanks."

☐ The Eucharist is one of the sacraments.

☐ A sacrament is an action of Jesus Christ who comes to be with us in the Church through the power of the Holy Spirit.

Family Time

Read together the Scripture story found on pages 14 and 15.

19

We Remember and Celebrate

With our Church community, we sing and delight in God's gifts. Gather into a circle to pray and sing together.

**O come, let us sing to the Lord.
Let us make a joyful noise!
Rejoice in the Lord always,
again I say rejoice!
Let us come into the Lord's
presence giving thanks!
Rejoice in the Lord always,
again I say rejoice!
Let us make a joyful noise to
him with songs of praise!
Rejoice in the Lord always,
again I say rejoice!**

Based on Psalm 95:1–2

Re - joice in the Lord ___ al - ways,

A - gain I say re - joice!

Let's Pray as One

Help your child see how family life is similar to our celebration of the Eucharist. Fold and staple blank paper together to make a booklet, using one page for each of the categories below. Draw or write about the times each of these happens in family life. Then invite your child to take the booklet to church once and help him or her identify when these occur at Mass.

Gather together

My family visits each other.

1) gather together
2) share stories about the past and present
3) prepare a meal
4) remember
5) share food
6) go to serve others

Let's Pray as One

Lucy stroked the baby's hand. He was her new cousin, who had just arrived from far away. He would be adopted and become part of Lucy's family forever.

"Does God want this baby to be ours?" she thought. "Is God here now?"

Grandmother touched Lucy's shoulder. She said, "Let's pray together. Thank you, God, for this baby. May we be a good family."

"Amen!" Lucy said.

She knew they could celebrate birthdays and Christmas together. They would go to church with friends to praise God, for they were all children of God.

The baby reached for Lucy's finger.

Use the code to find the mystery word.

| A 1 | B 2 | C 3 | D 4 | E 5 | F 6 | G 7 | H 8 | I 9 |

| J 10 | K 11 | L 12 | M 13 | N 14 | O 15 | P 16 | Q 17 | R 18 |

| S 19 | T 20 | U 21 | V 22 | W 23 | X 24 | Y 25 | Z 26 |

We are all God's __ __ __ __ __ __ __ __ .

3 8 9 12 4 18 5 14

Living as One

Long ago, the followers of Jesus prayed each day with one another. They ate together, talking about the miracles worked through the apostles. They divided up their money and clothing, sharing with everyone. More people joined them each day.

One day when they broke the bread and shared it with one another, a man said, "Jesus asked us to do this and remember him."

The others nodded.

"Praise God the Father who sent him to us!" a woman cried out. "Praise Jesus and praise his Spirit who blesses us now!"

Everyone smiled and began to sing. They knew Jesus was with them.

Based on Acts 2:42–44

How We Thank God

At Mass we thank God together as his people. We praise God as Father, Son, and Holy Spirit. We hear the word of God read to us from the Bible.

We pray with one another. We pray for one another and our Church leaders, the pope, and bishops. We are one with the followers of Jesus on earth and those in heaven.

We pray to God to help us love him more. We ask him for the gift of his life and love, called grace. Grace gives each of us the very life of Jesus. It makes us sons and daughters of the Father. It joins us together in the life of Jesus and all creation.

We bring gifts of bread and wine. By the power of the Holy Spirit, these gifts will become the Body and Blood of Christ.

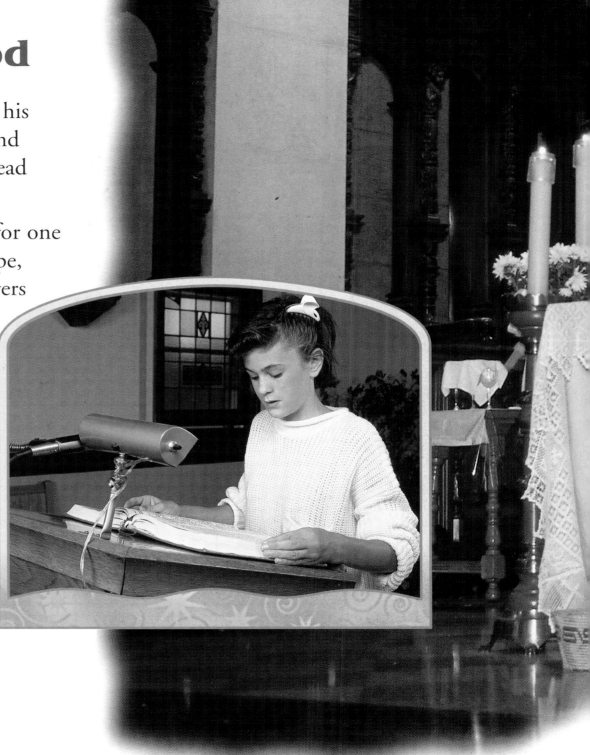

When we come together to give God thanks and praise for all he has done for us, he gives us even more! In the Eucharist he gives us the Body and Blood of Jesus Christ, his only Son, our Lord.

Jesus died on the cross to save us from our sins. This is why we call our celebration of the Eucharist a sacrifice. The word <u>sacrifice</u> means "a special gift given out of love." All of these prayers and actions at Mass make up one complete celebration.

Three in One

We often start prayers with the Sign of the Cross.

In the name of the Father,
and of the Son,
and of the Holy Spirit. Amen.

This sign shows us that God is three Persons in one. We always praise God as the Father, the Son, and the Holy Spirit.

Find and circle the words below.

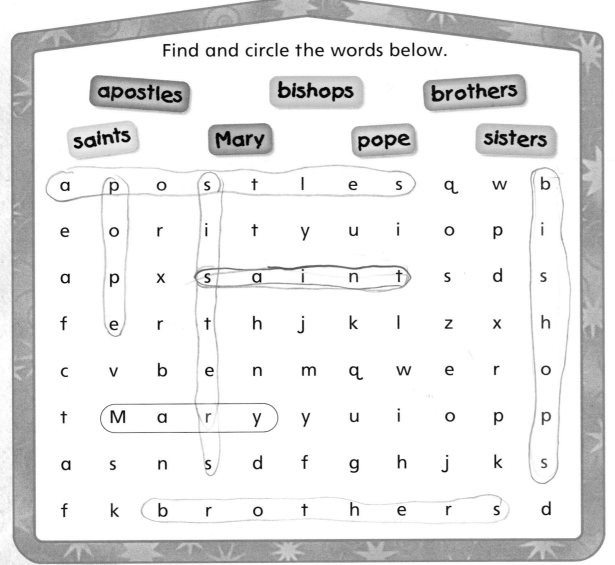

apostles   bishops   brothers

saints   Mary   pope   sisters

a	p	o	s	t	l	e	s	q	w	b
e	o	r	i	t	y	u	i	o	p	i
a	p	x	s	a	i	n	t	s	d	s
f	e	r	t	h	j	k	l	z	x	h
c	v	b	e	n	m	q	w	e	r	o
t	M	a	r	y	y	u	i	o	p	p
a	s	n	s	d	f	g	h	j	k	s
f	k	b	r	o	t	h	e	r	s	d

Family Time

Pray every day as a family and begin each prayer with the Sign of the Cross.

At Mass we pray with others and for others. We pray with and for those who are near us, those who are far away, and those who lived long ago.

We Believe

- ☐ Grace is God's gift of his life and love.
- ☐ We pray together to give thanks to God at Mass.
- ☐ We pray to God with and for one another and all the followers of Jesus on earth and in heaven.
- ☐ God is three Persons in one: the Father, the Son, and the Holy Spirit.

29

We Remember and Celebrate

Let's praise God who is three in one: the Father, the Son, and the Holy Spirit. Let's use our voices, our arms, our legs, and our hands. Let the color and movement of our ribbons and streamers show our praise. Let's celebrate how great God is!

We rejoice in God, the Creator and Father, who gives us life!
We rejoice in Jesus, the Son, whose love saves us!
We rejoice in the Holy Spirit, who breathes God's strength into our lives!

There is one God, one holy, wonderful God who gives us all that we need and more.
In the name of the Father, and of the Son, and of the Holy Spirit. Amen.

4
Family Time

The Gift of Gathering as the Community

Suggestions

- ☐ List people to invite.
- ☐ Draw a picture of the celebration you want.
- ☐ Decorate a photograph album obtained just for this occasion.
- ☐ Create invitations.
- ☐ Plan a menu of the food you will share together.
- ☐ Prepare a book or design a sheet of paper for your guests to sign.

Whether simple or elaborate, the celebration of your child's first Eucharist will be a special gathering, even if there are only two of you. Together, enjoy preparing for this celebration by using the suggestions to the left.

The Gift of Gathering as the Community

When you go to church, you give thanks and praise to God with other people. Some you know well. Some you know a little. Some you might like to meet.

Show your community celebrating together at Mass.
Draw faces and add the names of people at your
church. Don't forget to add your family and yourself!

Gathering with Jesus

$\mathbb{P}$eter hurled the heavy fishing net into the water. Would he catch any fish today?

His brother Andrew said, "Look, someone is coming!"

Jesus was on shore. He called, "Follow me, and you will fish for people."

Right away, they left their boat to go with him.

Further down the shore, James and John were with their father, Zebedee. They were mending their nets. Jesus called to them, "Come with me."

And right away, they too left their boat, to be with Jesus.

Based on Matthew 4:18–22

We Gather at Our Parish Church

The Lord calls us to himself, and so we gather together as the People of God. Part of the Holy Spirit's work in the celebration is to unite us in one voice. The priest greets us, "The Lord be with you." We answer, "And also with you."

Next, we pray together. We might ask God for his forgiveness and healing so that we can be reconciled with one another. Or we might remember our Baptisms and be sprinkled with holy water. No matter how we do it, we begin our celebration of thanksgiving by gathering together as the People of God.

On Sundays, we praise God: the Father, the Son, and the Holy Spirit. We are always loved by the Lord. We raise our voices in praise.

We Praise God

Sometimes the song we sing is the Gloria. This is a very old hymn of praise to Jesus Christ, our Lord.

Glory to God in the highest,
and peace to his people on earth.

These are the words that the angels sing in the Bible story about the birth of Jesus.

Unscramble the letters to form words and complete each sentence.

At the beginning of Mass, we (gnis) <u>sing</u>.

The priest (trgsee) <u>greets</u> us with the words "The Lord be with you." We (swrnae) <u>answer</u>, "And also with you." Together we (seairp) <u>praise</u> the Lord by singing the Gloria.

At Mass we use senses, feelings, and thoughts. All of these are gifts from God. Fill in the blanks below with words that describe how you use your feelings, thoughts, and senses.

At Mass, I

see _Jesus on the cross and people_.

hear _people sing_.

smell _wine from people's mouth_.

touch _the gold cup of wine_.

taste _____.

feel _Jesus and God all around us_

think of _Jesus on the cross_.

Family Time

As a family, go to church this Sunday to celebrate the Eucharist together.

We Believe

- ☐ Christ calls us together.
- ☐ The Holy Spirit unites us.
- ☐ Together we give thanks and praise to God who always loves us and forgives us.

We Remember and Celebrate

A litany is a number of short prayers of praise or prayers that ask God for something. Write a litany and pray it.

**We come together to pray
for those we love.**

Jesus, call _____

(name)

to you and to us.

**Gather us as your people.
Thank you, Lord, for the gift of
being able to gather as
a Church community.
Thank you for being with us. Amen!**

The Gift of God's Word to Us

Jesus taught with stories. At Mass, we still hear these, as well as other Bible readings. But in today's world of visual media, our children need to develop skills for listening to Scripture. On the lines below, add your own favorite Bible stories to the list of those from the book. Enjoy these Scripture stories together!

Place an X by the story that you want to hear.

☐ **The Birth of Jesus** (pages 4 and 5)

☐ **More Than Enough** (pages 14 and 15)

☐ **Living as One** (pages 24 and 25)

☐ **Gathering with Jesus** (pages 34 and 35)

☐ _____

_____

_____

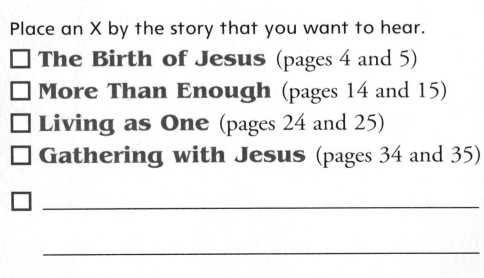

The Gift of God's Word to Us

Once there was a boy who couldn't see well. So he listened. He heard birds chirping, waves lapping, parents calling children, and a piano playing. He heard laughter and crying and praying.

Mostly, he heard stories.

The stories told him of things that were good and bad, funny and sad, wise and foolish. He learned how to love, how to treat others fairly, and how to make good choices. He did not look with his eyes, but with his heart, because he listened.

These words describe sounds. What do they mean to you? Write about each one.

Example:
swings creaking: pumping the swing high, wind blowing

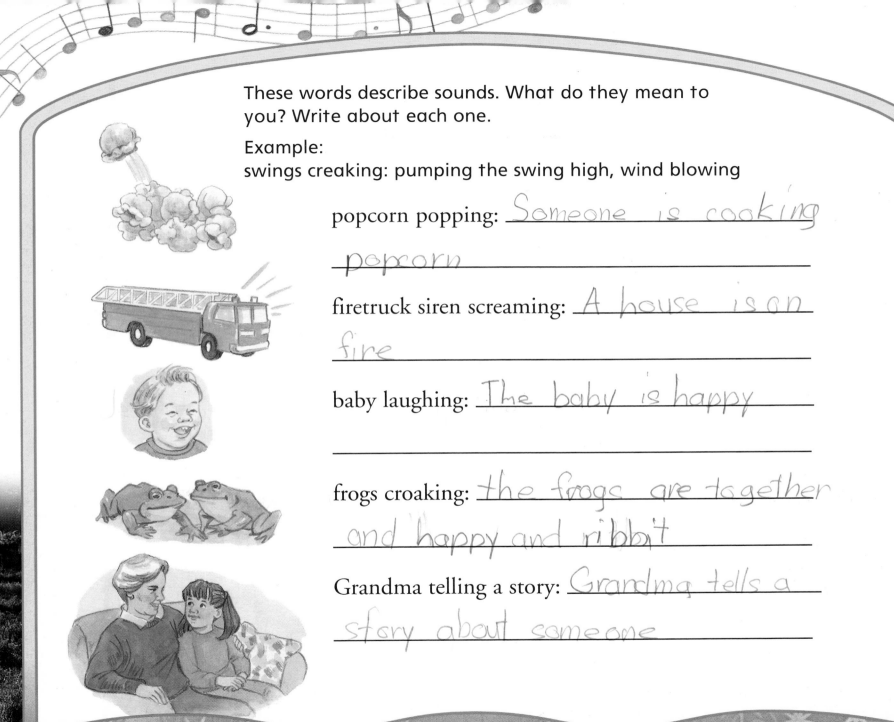

popcorn popping: _Someone is cooking popcorn_

firetruck siren screaming: _A house is on fire_

baby laughing: _The baby is happy_

frogs croaking: _the frogs are together and happy and ribbit_

Grandma telling a story: _Grandma tells a story about someone_

Jesus Reads from a Scroll

Jesus went to pray with others in his town. It was his turn to read. He stood up and a man placed a scroll in his hands. On the scroll were the words of the long-ago prophet Isaiah.

Jesus read, "The Spirit of the Lord is upon me. He chose me to bring good news to the poor. He sent me to free the captives. He called me to give sight to the blind and to help those who are not treated justly."

Then Jesus said, "What you just heard me read has come true today."

Based on Luke 4:16–21

Hearing the Word of God

At Mass, we hear Bible readings and know the Lord is with us. The Bible, also called Scripture, is the word of God. It is a gift from God and a way that he speaks to us. This part of our eucharistic celebration is called the Liturgy of the Word.

We hear the word of God read to us. We feel the power of the Holy Spirit, touching our hearts and giving us joy. God's love can change our relationships with him, with others, and with all creation. So we sing a song from the Bible, called a psalm.

The most important reading is the Gospel. It tells us about Jesus. Gospel means "good news." Hearing the good news of Jesus is so wonderful, we sing, "Alleluia!" This word means "Praise the Lord." The priest or deacon reads the Gospel. We hear about God's terrific promises and gifts for us.

We hear God's call to live justly and serve others. At the end of the Gospel, the priest or deacon says, "The gospel of the Lord." We answer, "Praise to you, Lord Jesus Christ."

The priest or deacon speaks to us. His words are called a homily. His words help us to treasure the readings and give thanks.

Next, we stand as one and declare what we believe. The creed tells the story of how Jesus saves us. It also tells us about God's love for us from the beginning of time to the end of time. This is called the Profession of Faith. Then we pray for ourselves and others during the Prayer of the Faithful.

A Gentle Storyteller

Blessed Kateri Tekakwitha was a Native American who loved Jesus greatly. She was born in 1656, and she died in 1680.

Kateri lay on her bed, very sick. She remembered the Scripture stories her mother had told her long ago. These helped her live a good life.

Two children came in, asking, "A story, please?"

Kateri smiled. "I'll tell you a story about Jesus that my mother told me," she said.

The children moved closer to listen.

What story about Jesus would you want Kateri to tell? What is your favorite Scripture story?

Draw a picture about it. Then write one sentence about what you have learned from it.

We learned that Jesus die

onte the cross.

Family Time

Have members of your family retell and talk about a Scripture story you heard at Mass recently.

We Believe

- ☐ The Bible, also called Scripture, is the word of God.

- ☐ Scripture is a gift from God and a way that he speaks to us.

- ☐ The Lord is with us when the word of God is heard and read.

- ☐ The most important reading, the Gospel, tells us about Jesus.

- ☐ The word <u>gospel</u> means "good news."

We Remember and Celebrate

In this celebration we show honor and respect for the word of God, the Bible. We put our Bible in a special place. We remember and celebrate the Bible stories we know and love. We thank God for his word to us. Whenever we read from the Bible, God is with us.

**Like the angels and shepherds,
     we thank you, God, for sending
          Jesus to us.**

**Like Philip and Andrew,
     we ask you, Father, to help us give
          thanks for the gift of Jesus.**

**Like Peter, James, and John,
     may we hear Jesus calling us.**

**Like the first Christians,
     we pray that we may live in Jesus' love.**

Lord, hear our prayer. Amen.

The Gift of Christ's Body and Blood

Make your child's First Eucharist a special memory! Together make a First Eucharist memory book, using a decorative blank notebook or an attractive binder and paper. Invite godparents, siblings, relatives, and friends to share memories of their own First Eucharist or to offer prayers and good wishes for your child. Your child can complete his or her own page reflecting on the eucharistic celebration to come.

People I would like to have sign my First Eucharist memory book:

_____

_____

_____

_____

_____

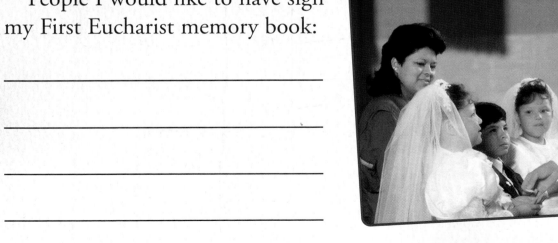

The Gift of Christ's Body and Blood

We remember happy, sad, scary, silly, and angry times. We remember people we love who are not with us and places we miss. Our memories are important to us. What are your favorite memories?

Complete the following sentences.

I was the sickest when _____

_____ .

The most frightening thing was _____

_____ .

I got hiccups when _____

_____ .

The funniest thing that ever happened to me was

_____

_____

_____.

My best birthday was _____

_____

_____.

I felt sad when _____

_____

_____.

The Last Supper

The night before he died, Jesus and his friends gathered for their meal.

Jesus' friends watched as he took the bread, blessed it, and broke it into pieces. He gave the bread to them. He said, "Take and eat. This is my body which is given for you."

All his friends ate.

54

Next to Jesus was a cup filled with wine.
Jesus picked up this cup, gave thanks, and gave
it to them.

"Take this and drink from it," Jesus said.
"This is the cup of my blood which will be
shed for you for the forgiveness of sins. Do this
in memory of me."

Based on Matthew 26:26–28

Special Gifts for Us

When we celebrate the Eucharist, we bring gifts of bread and wine to the altar. The altar is the table of the Lord. Here we do what Jesus told us to do.

This part of the Mass is called the Liturgy of the Eucharist. The priest acts in the name of Jesus. In Jesus' name, the priest prays the Eucharistic Prayer to God our Father for us.

In this great prayer, we join with the priest to remember all that Jesus did to save us. We remember his death and resurrection. We remember what Jesus did and said at the Last Supper. And then something wonderful happens.

By the power of the Holy Spirit, our gifts of bread and wine become the Body and Blood of Christ. This is Jesus, God's gift for us.

We pray the Our Father together to show our love and trust in God. We ask God to take care of us. We ask God to forgive our sins. We share a sign of peace to show we love one another and are united with one another. We do these things because God's gifts to us bring us closer to him.

Jesus died on the cross to save us from our sins. This is why we say the Eucharist is a sacrifice, or a special gift given out of love. Jesus offers himself to his Father for us. At this most special meal of the Eucharist, we receive God's gift of his Son with thanks and praise.

Receiving Communion

The gift of Jesus to us is so wonderful! Jesus invites us to receive Communion every time we attend Mass. We should not eat or drink anything but water for one hour before receiving Communion.

The priest, deacon, or eucharistic minister will say, "The Body of Christ." Answer "Amen." You may choose to receive Communion in your hand or on your tongue.

You may also receive from the chalice, or cup. The priest, deacon, or eucharistic minister will say, "The Blood of Christ." Answer "Amen." Take the chalice in both hands and sip carefully from it.

Why do we answer "Amen"? This word means "it is true." You are saying, "Yes, this is Jesus."

Color the spaces numbered 1 blue, 2 red, and 3 yellow.

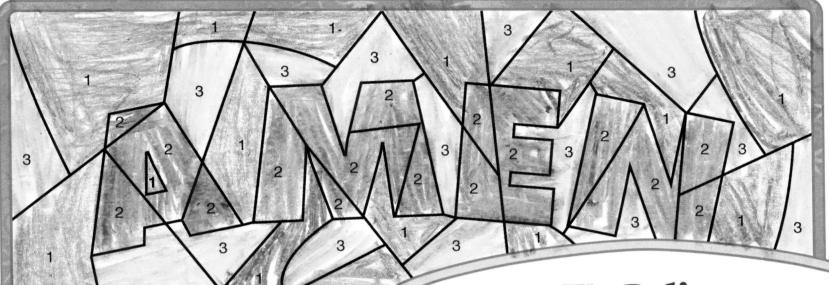

We Believe

- [ ] We bring gifts of bread and wine to the altar, which is the table of the Lord.

- [ ] In the Eucharistic Prayer, we remember all the wonderful things God has done for us.

- [ ] By the power of the Holy Spirit, our gifts of bread and wine become the Body and Blood of Christ.

- [ ] The Eucharist, a sacrifice and a most special meal, is God's gift to us.

Family Time

Read together the story of the Last Supper on pages 54–55.

We Remember and Celebrate

Soon you will be receiving Jesus in the Eucharist for the first time. This will be a special day. Do you feel a holy, happy quietness when you think about this? If you do, you are feeling reverent. We come to the table of the Lord with reverence and with so much joy! Think of one another as you prepare for this special day. To pray, use your hands and arms as well as your voice.

Jesus, as we prepare to receive you,
(Cup your hands together.)

we offer ourselves to you.
(Raise your cupped hands up.)

We offer you our hearts.
(Place your hands over your heart.)

We offer you our hands.
(Hold your hands out, palms up.)

We offer you our voices.
(Cup your mouth in your hands.)

These are our gifts to you.
(Raise your hands up.)

Jesus, please bless us all.
(Hold hands with one another.)

Amen.

The Gift of Serving Others

Strengthened by the Eucharist, we are called to share the gifts we have received by serving others. How can your family share God's love with others?

Be realistic, yet creative. Skip a favorite food or dessert for three days and give the money saved to a hunger-relief program. Help a neighbor. Send a get-well card to someone who is ill. Call or write a legislator about an injustice.

Walk

humbly

Love

tenderly

Color the letters of the words to show what the Lord asks of you.

Do

Justice

This is what the Lord asks of you:
Do justice,
love tenderly,
and walk humbly with your God.

Based on Micah 6:8

The Gift of Serving Others

$\mathbb{E}$very day, you have chances to care for others as God cares for you. When you give fresh water to a pet, make someone laugh, tie a younger child's shoe, or set the table for dinner, you are caring for others.

Look at the pictures. Mark the things you already do. Color in the circles of the ones you would like to do. Or write about what you can do.

_____

_____

Jesus the Servant

At the Last Supper, Jesus gave us his Body and Blood. He also taught us something else to remember.

Jesus looked at his friends, whom he loved so much. He tied a towel around his waist and poured water into a bowl. He knelt down and began washing the dirty, dusty feet of his friends. Then he wiped their feet dry with the towel.

His friends were shocked. They knew Jesus was much greater than they were. Now he was acting like a servant!

Peter said, "Do not do this!"

"You call me teacher and master, and yet I wash your feet," Jesus said. "Now you'll understand and be servants to each other, as I have been a servant to you."

Based on John 13:1–16

Together at the Table

In the Eucharist, we eat and drink together at the table of the Lord. The Body and Blood of Christ is the food and drink God gives us. God forgives our sins and makes us his people. The Eucharist is a gift for us. The Holy Spirit makes us one with the Lord. Christ is with us.

In the Eucharist, we are changed by the Holy Spirit. We are a people filled with God's grace and love. We experience hope. We remember that Jesus washed the feet of his disciples. He asks us to serve others. We remember that Jesus suffered and died for us. He asks us to help those who are suffering today.

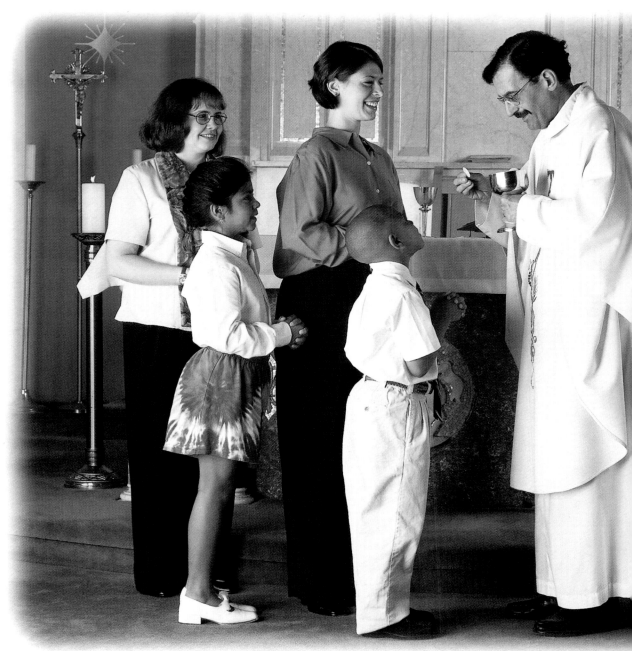

At the end of Mass, the priest blesses us. We can go to share the Lord's love with others! The priest says, "Go in peace to love and serve the Lord." With joy for all God's gifts to us, we respond, "Thanks be to God."

So we want to spread his peace to the world. We want to work for justice. We want to help those who are hurting. The gifts we have been given are to be given away.

Sharing God's Love

Do Justice

Saint Hedwig was a rich woman in Poland who shared her money, clothes, and food. During a war, Hedwig went with her husband to battle. There she talked with soldiers to stop the fighting. She helped make fair rules for her country.

Love Tenderly

Saint Vincent de Paul was a French priest who loved people. He cared for sick people, hungry people, babies who had no parents, and frightened children. He taught others to love and care for the poor people as he did.

Walk Humbly with God

Saint Isidore of Spain was a farmer's helper. He plowed and prayed. A good man, he saw God everywhere. He saw God in plants, in animals, and in the hungry people he helped. Some say angels helped him plow so that he could pray!

These saints shared in God's gift of Eucharist and were changed by the Holy Spirit. Think about their stories. Then answer the following questions.

Which of these stories do you like best?

I like the one that says love Tenderly

Why do you like the story?

Because it is talking about to love others

How can you be like one of these people?

Helping and careing.

Family Time

Think of little ways you can serve members of your family by being more patient, more forgiving, and more generous.

We Believe

☐ Our sins are forgiven at the table of the Lord.

☐ In the Eucharist, we are a people filled with God's grace and love.

☐ Jesus asks us to serve those who are suffering.

We Remember and Celebrate

We are all called to serve others. Each one of us has gifts. God wants us to share our gifts for the good of everyone.

Name a gift that you have. Thank God for this gift. Then pray together for God's blessing.

Lord, we are your people who believe in you.

May we always enjoy the gift of your love.

May we share your love with others.

Help us to serve others every day.

In the name of the Father, and of the Son, and of the Holy Spirit. Amen.

8
Family Time

The Gift of Everlasting Life

Jesus promised us the gift of everlasting life. We look forward to a future with Jesus and everyone else in the kingdom of God. At Mass, we get glimpses of the joy we will have. Through the lives of the saints, we also have a hint about what this will be like.

In the spaces below, invite your child to write the names of some of those saints about whom she or he has learned.

The Gift of Everlasting Life

At birthday parties, Joel's older cousin Zach always brought in the cake. He lit the candles, singing loudly, "Happy Birthday!"

Today the family celebrated the first birthday of Joel's sister. With them was someone new, Theresa. She and Zach would soon marry.

"Time for cake!" Grandpa called out.

Everyone looked at Zach.

Zach said, "It's time for me to give up my job. Now it's Joel's turn."

Joel lit the candle. He understood Zach was changing and growing.

So was Joel. He sang loudly, "Happy Birthday!"

Like Joel, we change and grow. We look to our future. On the roots of this flower, write things you learned when you were young (such as learning to talk). On the leaves, write something you are learning now (such as reading). On the petals, write what you might learn when you are older.

_____

_____   _____

The Greatest Celebration of All

Long ago, God spoke to a man named Isaiah about the future God planned for his people. We can read what Isaiah wrote about this in the Bible.

Isaiah explains that the time to come will be wonderful! It will be as wonderful as God inviting us to a great feast of rich and delicious food. Isaiah said it would be as amazing as eating sweet cakes, crusty breads, tasty cheeses, juicy peaches, and drinking cold, clear water. God will gather his people together for this marvelous celebration.

There will be no more sadness. God will wipe away any tears we have. Fighting, fear, and war will be no more. The world will be completely changed.

And with no sadness, how we will rejoice!

How great our God is! How happy we are
that God will do all this for us!

Based on Isaiah 25:6–9

75

A Wonderful Promise

At the end of time, Jesus will come again. He invites us to be with him and our heavenly Father forever in the kingdom of God. This is the Lord's promise to us of everlasting life.

Today, we see a little about what the kingdom of God will be like. We know the joy of being with Jesus when we read the Bible, when we do good things for one another, and when we sing and pray together.

At Mass, the Holy Spirit gathers us as the Church of Jesus, the Body of Christ, the People of God. We eat and drink together at the table of the Lord. The Lord Jesus comes to us throughout the celebration. He comes to us in the words of Scripture. He comes to us when we receive his Body and Blood in Communion. He is with us when we share God's gifts by serving others. He is with us when we live justly.

On the glorious day to come, there will be no more death or sadness, no more crying or pain. There will be love, peace, and happiness forever. We will know the greatest joy there is—to be with God!

Find and circle the following words.

Scripture   serve   Eucharist

Gathers   Community   justly

```
W  C  V  B  N  M  Z  X  C  A  S
A  C  O  M  M  U  N  I  T  Y  D
L  F  G  H  J  K  L  Q  W  E  G
J  R  S  T  Y  U  I  O  P  A  A
U  S  E  U  C  H  A  R  I  S  T
S  C  R  I  P  T  U  R  E  T  H
T  D  V  F  G  H  J  K  L  Z  E
L  B  E  C  V  B  N  M  Q  W  R
Y  E  R  T  Y  U  I  O  P  A  S
C  S  D  F  G  H  J  K  Z  V  B
```

On the rainbow, write the names of people you would like to meet in the kingdom of God. Then complete the sentence below,

In the kingdom of God, I think people will feel

_____

_____.

We Believe

☐ Jesus invites us to be with him in the kingdom of God.

☐ At Mass, we see a little about what life will be like in the kingdom of God.

☐ Everlasting life means being with God forever.

☐ To be with God forever is the greatest joy of all.

Family Time

Take a moment with your family to rejoice in all the good things in your life. As each one of these is named, answer joyfully, "Thanks, God!"

We Remember and Celebrate

Jesus promised that he will be with us when two or three of us gather in his name. We often gather together in his name with our parish community, our families, and our classmates and friends. We remember the wonderful gifts Jesus gives us. Our hearts fill with joy. We give the Lord thanks and praise.

Make paper chains to celebrate all God's gifts. On each link, write one gift for which you are thankful. Hang the paper chain where you can see it. Pray together the prayer below in thanks and praise.

Shout joyfully to the Lord.

Praise God with gladness.

Come into his presence singing.

Based on Psalm 100:1–2

After the Celebration: Let's Follow Jesus

The excitement of First Eucharist may be over, but your child's eucharistic life has only begun. Like the apostle Paul, who wrote encouraging letters to the early Christians, you too can encourage your child. Think of your child's gifts, such as humor, generosity, joyfulness, insight, and helpfulness. Your child is a unique individual, whose very presence is one of God's most wonderful gifts. Write your child a note of encouragement.

Paste a photograph
of your First Communion here.

Dear _____,

Let's Follow Jesus

There was a man named Saul who looked for people who loved Jesus and put them in jail. One day, Saul was going to a town to look for Christians. Suddenly, the sky was filled with a light. It was so bright that Saul fell to the ground. He heard a voice say, "Saul, Saul, why do you hurt me?"

It was Jesus calling him.

At that moment, Saul believed in Jesus. Saul was changed. So he took a new name, Paul.

Paul traveled far and wide, teaching people about Jesus. He wrote many letters to help the first Christians. Here is what he told them.

Blessings and peace to you!

I thank God for you. It's wonderful that you are part of our community and receiving Eucharist!

Friends, you are made strong in the Holy Spirit.
Be caring as Jesus cares for you. Be brave. Do good
deeds, all in the name of love.

Based on Acts of the Apostles 9:1–19

83

Growing and Changing

You are a gift to others from God. You have the chance to share his love. There is so much you can do and be. Just as Paul changed, the Holy Spirit can help you to be a better person, too. When you receive the Eucharist, you become richer in God's gifts. Sharing these gifts with others is the best way to give God thanks.

Find your way through the maze to Jesus. Notice the flowers growing along the way.

Keep Off
—
Seeds Planted

START
HERE

Family Time

Share with your child a story about a time when he or she was little. Tell your child how proud you are of him or her now.

We Remember and Celebrate

Paul said that each of us has many gifts, all given to us by the Holy Spirit. Think about the people who are special to you. Draw a picture of these special people on a sheet of paper. Then thank God for these people by reading these words from Scripture.

There are many gifts, but one Holy Spirit. There are many kinds of work, but all is done for the same God. His Spirit works in different ways in different people, but it is the same God who is working in all of us.

Based on 1 Corinthians 12:4–7

We Celebrate at the Lord's Table

We gather together to give the Lord thanks and praise.

> Priest: In the name of the Father,
> and of the Son,
> and of the Holy Spirit.
>
> People: Amen.
>
> Priest: The Lord be with you.
>
> People: And also with you.

We pray together as the People of God. We might pray,

> Priest or deacon: Lord, have mercy.
>
> People: Lord, have mercy.
>
> Priest or deacon: Christ, have mercy.
>
> People: Christ, have mercy.
>
> Priest or deacon: Lord, have mercy.
>
> People: Lord, have mercy.

We raise our voices in praise to the Lord.

> Glory to God in the highest,
> and peace to his people on earth.
>
> Lord God, heavenly King,
> almighty God and Father,
> we worship you, we give you thanks,
> we praise you for your glory.
>
> Lord Jesus Christ, only Son of the Father,
> Lord God, Lamb of God,
> you take away the sin of the world:
> have mercy on us;
> you are seated at the right hand of
> the Father:
> receive our prayer.
>
> For you alone are the Holy One,
> you alone are the Lord,
> you alone are the Most High,
> Jesus Christ,
> with the Holy Spirit,
> in the glory of God the Father. Amen.

We hear several readings from Scripture.

> Reader: The word of the Lord.

> People: Thanks be to God.

We stand for the most important reading of all, the Gospel.

> People: Alleluia!

The priest or deacon reads the Gospel.

> Priest or deacon: The gospel of the Lord.

> People: Praise to you, Lord Jesus Christ,

We declare what we believe. The creed tells the story of how Jesus saves us. It also tells us about God's love for us from the beginning of time to the end of time. The creed begins,

> We believe in one God,
>   the Father, the Almighty,
>   maker of heaven and earth,
>   of all that is seen and unseen.

We pray for ourselves and others during the Prayer of the Faithful.

> All: Lord, hear our prayer.

We bring gifts of bread and wine to the altar. The priest asks God to bless the bread that will become Jesus.

> People: Blessed be God forever.

> Priest: Pray, brethren, that our sacrifice may be acceptable to God, the almighty Father.

> People: May the Lord accept the sacrifice at your hands for the praise and glory of his name, for our good, and the good of all his Church.

The Eucharistic Prayer begins.

Priest: The Lord be with you.

People: And also with you.

Priest: Lift up your hearts.

People: We lift them up to the Lord.

Priest: Let us give thanks to the Lord
our God.

People: It is right to give him thanks
and praise.

With joy in our hearts, we praise God.

All: Holy, holy, holy Lord, God of power
and might.

Heaven and earth are full of your glory.

Hosanna in the highest.

Blessed is he who comes in the name
of the Lord.

Hosanna in the highest.

In the Eucharistic Prayer we remember all that
Jesus did to save us. Through the power of the
Holy Spirit, the bread and wine become the
Body and Blood of Jesus Christ.

Priest: Let us proclaim the mystery
of faith.

People: Christ has died, Christ has risen,
Christ will come again.

We pray with and for our Church leaders
and one another in heaven and on earth. We
bless God.

Priest: Through him,
with him,
in him,
in the unity of the Holy Spirit,
all glory and honor is yours,
almighty Father,
forever and ever.

People: Amen.

Together we pray the prayer that Jesus taught us.

Our Father, who art in heaven,
hallowed be Thy name.
Thy kingdom come;
Thy will be done on earth
    as it is in heaven.

Give us this day our daily bread;
    and forgive us our trespasses
    as we forgive those
    who trespass against us;
    and lead us not into temptation,
        but deliver us from evil.

Amen.

We show that we are one, the People of God, at the Sign of Peace.

Priest: The peace of the Lord be with
    you always.

People: And also with you.

Priest or deacon: Let us offer each other
    the sign of peace.

We see the priest break the large host, which is the Body of Christ. We remember how Jesus broke the bread for his followers at the Last Supper.

People: Lamb of God, you take away the
    sins of the world:
        have mercy on us.

Lamb of God, you take away the
    sins of the world:
        have mercy on us.

Lamb of God, you take away the
    sins of the world:
        grant us peace.

Priest: This is the Lamb of God
    who takes away the sins of
    the world.
    Happy are those who are called to
    his supper.

All: Lord, I am not worthy to receive you,
    but only say the word and I shall
    be healed.

We receive Jesus in the Eucharist.

Priest, deacon, or eucharistic minister:
   The Body of Christ.

Response: Amen.

Priest, deacon, or eucharistic minister:
   The Blood of Christ.

Response: Amen.

We receive God's blessing and go to share his love with others.

Priest: The Lord be with you.

People: And also with you.

Priest: May almighty God bless you, the Father, and the Son, and the Holy Spirit.

People: Amen.

Then we are sent to share the Lord's gifts to us.

Priest or deacon: Go in peace to love and serve the Lord.

People: Thanks be to God.

Chalice

Cruets

Book with Scripture readings

Hosts

Paten

Crucifix

Tabernacle

Easter candle

Altar

Ambo

Glossary

Baptism is one of the sacraments of initiation into the family of Jesus' Church when God first blesses us with the gift of new life.

Bible is the word of God. It is a way God speaks to us. It is also called the Scriptures.

Catholic Church is the People of God, who are led by the pope and bishops.

Confirmation is one of the sacraments of initiation that strengthens the new life that the Holy Spirit gives us at Baptism. The Holy Spirit helps us to live as Jesus did, to tell others about Jesus, and to serve others.

Creed tells the story of how Jesus saves us. It tells us about God's love for us from the beginning of time until the end of time.

Eucharist is one of the sacraments of initiation. The Eucharist, a sacrifice and a special meal of thanks, is God's gift to us.

In the Eucharist, God gives the Body and Blood of Jesus to make us his people.

Gospel means "good news."

Grace gives us the very life of Jesus. It makes us the sons and daughters of the Father. It joins us together in the life of Jesus and all creation.

Homily the priest's or deacon's words about the Scripture readings

Kingdom of God the Lord's promise of everlasting life where there will be great joy and no sadness

Sacrament is a most special celebration. It is an action of Christ who comes to be with us in the Church through the power of the Holy Spirit.

Sacrifice is a special gift given out of love.